Freedom To Blaze Your Trail

Level Up Edition

Warrior Princess Nation, LLC

KEYS 2 VICTORY

Freedom To Blaze Your Trail
Level Up Edition

Presented By: Nakisha Woods

First Printing 2024

Published by Warrior Princess Nation, LLC
6935 Aliante Pkwy Ste 104-423 North Las Vegas, NV 89084
info@warriorprincessnation.com

Freedom To Blaze Your Trail

Introduction

I Am A Trailblazer   Pastor J. Mason

Chapter1
    Just G.O. (God Ordained)   Dawneshia Logo

Chapter 2
    The "Dai" I lost My Mind   Daishanai Jefferson

Chapter 3
    Trust In God   Chermeka Alexander

Chapter 4
    She Is Clothed In Strength and   Teiara Wortham
Dignity

Chapter 5
    Full Circle   ShaShanta Aldridge

Chapter 6
    Honor Your Yes   Nakisha Woods

Acknowledgements

Then I said, "I will not make mention of Him, Nor speak anymore in His name." But His word was in my heart like a burning fire Shut up in my bones; I was weary of holding it back, And I could not.
Jeremiah 20:9 NKJV

Introduction

I always knew, deep down in my soul and spirit, that I was called to be a leader, an innovator, and destined for greatness. When I began my healing work in 1999, during my pregnancy with my oldest child, I wanted everyone I knew to be set free. However, I did not truly understand the gifts that God had blessed me with. I would often meet people for the first time and have an instant, genuine connection with them. It was quite fascinating.

I noticed a trend as I continued to evolve into who the Lord destined for me to be. Almost every individual I spent time with, whether they had a problem, wanted to hit a goal, or just needed some encouragement, would leave my presence genuinely feeling uplifted.

Each of the phenomenal authors you will meet throughout the following pages has played such a pivotal role in me walking in my authority not only as an Apostle but as a Resilience Life Empowerment Coach and TrailBLAZHER!

According to www.dictionary.com a Trailblazer is defined as a person who blazes a trail for others to follow through unsettled country or wilderness; pathfinder.
A pioneer in any field of endeavor.

I can definitely relate to that definition. I have been a leader who continues to blaze her trail as a survivor of domestic violence (unsettled country), the first of my father's children to attend college (wilderness), and as a woman who helps adults obtain their high school diplomas and execute in all the benefits of the education system(pathfinder).

However, as we explore the word and take a look at the life of John the Baptist, in short, the Bible tells us about a "trailblazer," John the Baptist, who prepared people to meet and worship Jesus. He said, "Make ready the way of the Lord. Make his paths straight." He traveled around baptizing people and telling them about Jesus.

In the book of Mark, it reads:

As it is written in Isaiah the prophet: "I will send my messenger ahead of you, who will prepare your way" — "a voice of one calling in the wilderness, 'Prepare the way for the Lord, make straight paths for him.' Mark 1:2-3 NIV

Have you ever felt like a messenger? I truly have. It's one thing to feel like a messenger, but to walk in the FREEDOM of a messenger is entirely different. As I began to develop a deeper relationship with Christ, I heard the call upon my life. And accepted the call, the FREEDOM began to take residency in my inner spirit. As this FREEDOM began to capture my mind, body, soul, and spirit I asked God to allow me the ability to assist others in their FREEDOM. There was just one obstacle: I had never witnessed anyone operate how God was allowing me to operate. However, whom the Son set free is free indeed, so I relied totally upon the Holy Spirit to lead the way. Guess what? Holy Spirit did just that.

Pastor J. Mason
aka Yoke Breaker

I Am A Trailblazer

As I sit in my bed
locked in my head
I feel so drained
because of regret
For I fear what I can't get
without even trying

I'm like a car stuck in the mud
I fear I don't deserve love
there's a thief that kills
And it is all in my mind

I regret not realizing
Sooner who and what I am
God has opened my eyes
Chains have fallen off my mind

I am now aware I can succeed

Because God's love upholds me
I am a trailblazer no longer on
the porch of fear

I remove my crown of shame
And put on my crown of victory
ready to engage in life's beauty
to engage in my purpose
to succeed in all God has for me

Either walk with me or get out of my way
for I have finally awakened from the dream
of not being enough. My glass overflows
I am wonderfully and fearfully made

I'm suited up in the Favor of God
I have arrived; I realize that mountains
are not smooth yet, I shall climb them
For I am trail blazer moving forward

I shall never again sit back
wait on or fear success
For I am a Trail Blazer lineup
Look closely, and you will see
you too are
A TRAILBLAZER, just like me

Facebook: Pastor Juanita Mason Email: antelopeupperroomm@gmail.com
(916)792-4802 Pastor Mason Gospel Show on The Daily Gospel Show

Chapter 1

Dawneshia Logo

Just G.O. (God Ordained)

When I was almost 13 years old, my great Aunty Earma Jean told me, after I had performed with my praise dance team, "I looked at you and saw a yellow light or glow around you when you were dancing." I had no idea what she was talking about. I remember giggling and asking her if she really saw it or just said that. Back then, I was different from my sisters and friends and felt alone. As a child without context or someone to explain those feelings, I second-guessed myself. As I got older in high school, it manifested into low self-esteem and wondering if something was wrong with me. I've always been the one to move to the beat of my own drum throughout life, but back then, I didn't have the confidence to be okay and firm in my uniqueness.

I loved spending time with my great Aunty Earma. I would spend the night with her so I could go to church with her on Sundays. Around that time, my grandma bought me a portable CD player, and my Aunty Earma gifted me my first gospel CD by Mary Mary. Had I known what my Aunty was doing, that she was speaking and prophesying over me, I probably would have walked much taller and more confident during my teen years. I enjoyed going to church. I loved being a part of the youth ministry; it brought me a lot of joy and peace as a young person. So, when I was almost 14, I gave my life to Christ. I wanted to feel better within and everything around me to improve. It was tough as a young girl growing up in Oakland, CA, with my sisters and mom working and going to school.

I struggled not having my physical and biological father around. I questioned my self-worth and if I was worthy to be loved by him. I longed for him to be there for my sisters and me. My pastor said something so significant during service one Sunday. It was youth Sunday, so all the youth sat together in the first couple of pews to the right of the altar because we were leading in some parts of the service. Our pastor had us all stand up as he spoke and said, "If your physical father isn't in your life, you have a Father in Heaven who loves you, who cares for you, and that you can depend on Him." I remember tears rolling down my face and hearing my pastor or a voice I thought was my pastor say, "Keep standing." Little did I know it was really the Lord, and I was hearing His voice for the first time, and so clearly, might I add. I heard my pastor chuckle, and when I opened my eyes, all of my youth ministry friends had already sat down. Then my pastor said, "That's alright, keep standing; God loves you, little sister." That was the first time I inclined my ears to the Lord and the first step for me to "Just GO." It was a God-Ordained moment for me to begin breaking generational curses and being obedient to God's voice.

After I said yes to the Lord, I started struggling in school, more so with "friends," because I didn't want to do what they did anymore. I was called a church mouse, asked why I was always going to church, and made fun of because of that choice. Then, feeling pressured, I acted out in school by not doing my work. I got into my first real fight in 8th grade. I remember my mom being so upset and asking what was going on. I remember saying I wanted to be with my grandma. After being promoted from the 8th grade, I packed my bags and left Oakland with my grandma and Aunty Monique to go back to Sacramento that summer. The trouble that I got into was now a distant memory. It was a lot of memories I didn't care to hold on to. Although I would miss my mom, Aunty Earma, and sisters, I felt relief I could start fresh without this cloud hanging over my head. With me going into my first year of high school, away from my "friends," away from what I knew, I was excited to start anew. Initially, I was so sure of myself, but then situations changed. I was bullied about my looks and size, which had me questioning my worth. Experiencing these difficult and hurtful situations made me miss my sisters, mom, church family, and spending time with my Aunty Earma. I didn't know that I could pray without it being formal or fancy. I didn't know that I could talk to God like He was a friend/father because I didn't know what that relationship looked like. Instead, I clung to what brought me joy: listening to my gospel CDs, R&B, and pop groups. I even picked up the skill and hobby of decorating and customizing my spirit gear for school.

During football season at Grant High School, I was presented with the opportunity to join the Pacerettes. Around then, the Pacerettes team was starting again; they used to be around back in the day. We had some work to do to raise funds and secure uniforms, but I was so excited to join. When I asked my grandma and mom if I could join, the issue of money came up, and I started getting discouraged. I thought things would stop before they ever began. Back then, I didn't know who the Holy Spirit was, but something in me didn't let me give up. I kept pressing the issue until I got the okay. Throughout my childhood, opportunities to join sports programs or extracurricular activities were always stopped because of the money or how my siblings and I would get there because my mom worked hard and a lot. She worked hard to ensure we had a roof over our heads, clothes, shoes, and food in our bellies. I appreciate my mom because she did what she could. So many of those opportunities to be a part of teams weren't feasible then. As a fresh high school ninth grader, I didn't let that plague my mind; I heard "Just GO," so I did. My Aunty Monique had an In-Home daycare, and she gave me my first job helping with activities and schoolwork and paid me once a week. I used the money I earned to cover the expense of being a Pacerette and buy things I needed or wanted. That football season brought me many experiences and opportunities, but mostly, it taught me a lesson, "Just GO" and let nothing or no one detour you.

At the end of the first semester, I lost my Aunty Earma—the woman who planted seeds of love and prayer and taught me about loving the Lord. The woman who bought me my first gospel CD was gone. I remember doing my homework in the living room; my grandma was reading a book; she's a reader, always has been; it was 6:00 pm. She called my Aunty Earma, her baby sister, to ensure she was up for work. My grandma said, "She's not answering the phone, probably still sleeping. I don't want her to be late for work." So, she kept calling, and the phone kept ringing and ringing.

My grandma finally called my great-grandma because she lived with my Aunty Earma. My grandma asked her to go into the room to wake her up. My great-grandma came back and said that my Aunty wouldn't wake up. I remember my grandma yelling, "What?" really loudly, which startled me. I started asking my grandma what was going on, and then my grandma told my great-grandma, Mama, to dial 911. She told her, "I'm about to call Missy (my mom) to come over." I remember I ran to my room, fell to my knees, cried, and asked God a lot of questions, but mainly, I cried. When we returned to Oakland to help go through her room and box things, we found all these prayer letters under her mattress. My Aunty Earma had written two pages, front and back, of a prayer for my mom, sisters, and me. I believe it was her prayers that kept us going in the most difficult times.

The second half of the school year kind of went by really quickly and like a blur because I don't remember much towards the end of my 9th-grade year. I was still grieving, and I just wanted to get back to my mom and sisters. The remainder of my high school years were filled with ups and downs, trying to find myself, seek God, and figure out what a relationship with the Lord looked like. I moved back to Sacramento for my senior year, and after I graduated, my mom and sisters moved there as well. We lived next door to each other; my grandma purchased a new duplex house and owned both sides. I was so excited about graduating and thought of attending Berkeley Community College. My older cousin on my dad's side let me move with her. I got a job working at Subway and enjoyed this new life of independence. I loved myself and had this new-found confidence, and I loved that.

Usually, I walked to this liquor store right around the corner from the house my cousin and I lived in. I always walked there either before work or after work to get snacks. I would see a childhood friend hanging out with his buddies, and he would always tell the guys around there to respect me and not talk crazy, or if they saw me walking home late at night, they should walk with me to ensure I was safe. On one specific day, I had difficulty finding my house key; I was supposed to walk to the store and then head to work for a few hours. Unfortunately, when I found my key, it was time for me to go to work; no store run. I made it to work, and that day seemed unusually long, but I took it as God protecting me from something so much greater. Why else would my house key go missing? With me running late to work, I had to stay later to make up for missed time, and I was bummed. I wanted to hang out with my friends and then go home.

No one was out on the block when it was time to head home from work. I was used to seeing old childhood friends hanging out, but that evening, nothing. Once in the house, I got this call from my sister, telling me that an old childhood friend, the same childhood friend who made sure no one disrespected me, was shot and killed in front of the liquor store I always walked to. My mom had been urging me to come home for a while, but I loved my newfound independence. However, that incident threw me for a loop, and I felt like God needed me to leave and Just GO. It wasn't safe to be in that neighborhood anymore; it was time for me to take my belongings and go. I had gone through some drama with family on my dad's side, and it made me wonder about all those years that I longed to feel like I belonged. Maybe, after all, God was protecting me from that hurt and frustration.

When I turned nineteen, I remember feeling tired and overwhelmed. I started going back to church, building a relationship with the Lord, and on August 2, 2009, I was baptized. When I took the classes with my pastor, one of the youth leaders, and others getting baptized, I remember hearing them say when I got baptized, things would get rocky because Satan wants us to fall and go back to our past ways. It made me nervous, and I started thinking about all the ways the enemy would try me, but God reminded me of all the times that He kept me safe and loved on me even when I felt unworthy. Before I was baptized, I started dating a guy who initially seemed to be a great guy. I started feeling so low being with him. All my dreams and aspirations seemed like a distant memory when I was with him. When I chose to get baptized and started building my relationship with the Lord, that guy didn't like the changes I was making. All I knew was that God was calling me back to Him, back into His arms, and He needed me to let that guy go. God had given me clear instructions to Go, and I knew I had to obey. I knew that my life depended on it. My pursuit of living a life for Christ was all that mattered. So there I was, back hurting and frustrated because things didn't go my way. I started rebelling and ended up pregnant. In 2010, I discovered I was carrying a little girl, and I knew I didn't want those same cycles to repeat themselves. I knew I had to cling to God more than ever before because my life was changing drastically, and I was also birthing a new life. I started seeking the Lord more often, prayed more, and prepared to be a mom and bring a child into this world. My nights and days were spent writing a plan for my daughter and me. When I gave birth, so much went on around me that I only had enough energy for my daughter A'Jani and God.

Fast forward to A'Jani, now two years old. I was living with my mom, two sisters, and niece. I was going to work and school Monday through Friday, but I felt like I wasn't going anywhere and was losing precious time with my daughter. So, on the weekends, we spent a lot of time together doing whatever we wanted and going wherever we wanted within budget. I told myself I would never let money hinder us, especially my daughter. Around that time, I worked with the City of Sacramento's parks and recreation division in the after-school program world. An opportunity to work for the school district came around, but I didn't give any thought to it other than, "Do I really want to have more time away from my daughter?" When I brought it up to my sister in Christ and mentor, Coach Key, she encouraged me to apply so that I could get my foot in the door with the district. I had so many excuses I could have allowed to control my life and kept me stagnant, and I didn't want to be let down if I wasn't chosen. God is so funny in the way that He talks to me. I woke up out of my sleep to complete the application. The deadline was approaching soon. I had the experience because I worked in the city's after-school program. I uploaded all of my documents, and about a week after the job application closed, I received a call that I was selected for an interview at the district. Remember I stated that I went to school and worked Monday through Friday? I planned to pick up classes for the summer semester instead of a full class load during the Spring/Fall semesters so I could take the offer if given. There was a lady who worked at the preschool right across the field from the after-school program where I worked. I always said hi and conversed with her when she came to our school library with the preschoolers. This teacher saw me working with my students in the afterschool program Monday through Friday, leading, being engaged, and loving what I do. There was a panel when I walked through the door to the interview. This same teacher was sitting at the table during that interview. My heart skipped a beat, and I started smiling, thinking about when God woke me up to complete that application. Listen, when God says GO, just GO. That same week, I got a call that I had the job. I had no idea this teacher I said hi to EVERY DAY was the head of the preschool with two separate classrooms. So, with two jobs, my next goal was to get a place for my daughter and me.

I went to church more often and was being picked up occasionally by my co-worker or my site coordinator. An opportunity came about for a one-bedroom apartment in a low-income complex. It was so beautiful over there. I was told that I only needed three months of pay stubs, and I had received my 3rd pay stub from the school district. Some comments questioned whether I could afford to live independently and with A'Jani. After the apartment complex manager finished the calculations, I was told that I had met the requirements for the income limit and that the credit check was clear. My daughter and I moved into our place on Valentine's Day in 2014, and I was so overjoyed that I just cried when I walked into my new apartment. If I had listened and let the comments about income take root or control my thoughts, I would have missed out on my blessing. God told me to GO, and I had to "Just GO." I then learned that the church I would attend sometimes was also a 5 to 10-minute walk from our house, and my spirit leaped.

When I was pregnant with A'Jani and in labor with her, I promised God I would give her back to Him. I raised my daughter to be carefree and to love the Lord, so when we moved closer to church, I made it our home church and became a part of the youth ministry. A year before this, I created a girl's enrichment program called Queens of Purpose. I didn't know how it would be sustained, but I trusted God, and the people who were strategically placed in my life witnessed me "Just GO" (God Ordained); they donated their time, supplies and my home church donated the space so I could mentor the youth and teen girls there. I knew I had to do things differently for my baby girl, A'Jani. I created the space I longed for as a girl, and the Lord blessed the program. Not only did I mentor and speak life into the girls at my church, but that time also blessed me. The Lord showed me what a God-ordained and led lifestyle looked like and how it could bless all those around.

During all of this growth, increase in finance, and increase in territory, I met and dated my now husband. There was a time we separated when we were dating, and God told me, "I need your focus, I need your time, you're not ready yet." Listen, I cried like a baby, but I had to let GO, catch that. I believed God would bring us back together if it were meant to be. God said, 'Just GO", focus on what I'm calling you to do, and I promise I will give you the desires of your heart. Psalms 37:4 became a foundational Scripture for me.

There I was, living my life with my daughter, obeying the call, and healing. Then, at some point, the memories of that ex-boyfriend came and stayed with me. Those memories didn't bring tears or frustration; that's how I knew the Lord was showing me my prayers going forth. I used to pray and ask God to remove the pain. I didn't want to get upset with the memories or be triggered when his name came up. God loved me enough to help me heal through that, stand firm in my decision, and have faith that God had us (A'Jani, my now husband, and me) covered. In November 2014, I got a text from that same ex-boyfriend saying that God showed him our life as husband and wife, and by April 2015, he proposed. December 19, 2015, was our wedding. This love story, which I call our after-school love story, is filled with many testimonies of faith, abundance, testing, and growth. Our love story is a story all on its own for another book *wink wink*, but I trusted the Lord; I had to "Just GO," and by doing so, I broke so many generational curses. I said no to the negative cycles on my bloodline that will never touch OUR family.

I am a mother to five beautiful children. Even though my labor/birth with my first three children was traumatic, I said no to unhealthy cycles. God told me to seek a midwife in November of 2019 for my 4th pregnancy, and I gave birth to a beautiful, healthy, strong-willed girl in the birth center with only my midwives and my husband at the height of Covid in

April of 2020. When God told me to give birth at a birth center, my mother, mother-in-love, grandma, and my great-aunt all questioned my choices. I ignored their opinions and focused on what God told me to do. When hospitals were only allowing the birthing mother or when many were going to the hospitals sick and afraid to step foot into hospitals, only then did my family say they were thankful I wouldn't be giving birth in a hospital.

When God said, "Just GO," I knew He wouldn't steer me wrong. I felt so empowered after giving birth at a birth center, in water, after I was told eight months before by a nurse practitioner I wouldn't be able to give birth vaginally because my last birth was a c-section. Then I was told the risks but was never told the percentage of those risks or how much more of a risk it would be to have a repeat c-section. I knew that I didn't want to experience the pain of major surgery again, and I told the Lord, "There has to be another way." When God said, "Just GO," with a midwife, stay away from the hospitals, that empowered me to be confident as a mother, woman, and wife. It allowed my husband to see for himself even more the power of God in just being obedient. That empowering journey led me to become a doula. A doula supports/helps pregnant women informationally, emotionally, physically, and, in my case, spiritually as well because I am a doula who prays. My mission is to encourage and empower women and mothers in my community. I hit the ground running when God told me to Go; I had to "Just GO." I applied for scholarships two months after I had given birth to our 4th child. Three months later, the two organizations that made those scholarships available emailed me to let me know that I had won those scholarships. I started my training, and then I saw a course that was being offered that would be considered "continuing education." This course focused on studying herbs and nutrition for pre/post-natal care. I would try to figure out how to get the funds for that course, but I just went to God and asked. I talked to my sister-in-love about it, and a week before Christmas, before the deadline, she blessed me with half of that course fee as an early Christmas gift. When God says, Go, "Just Go."

I got my first client in January 2021; she gave birth on my son's 3rd birthday, and we built a great relationship. The following month, I applied for another partial scholarship for another doula training. A few weeks after applying, I was chosen for the scholarship. I know you're probably thinking, why would she apply for another training? To answer your question, I wanted to be well-equipped. Birth work constantly evolves; staying current with education and best practices is important. Also, I want to note that I was loud about my victories and my journey to becoming a doula. I grew comfortable with celebrating myself and doing it loudly. I wasn't playing small anymore, and anyone uncomfortable with it was none of my business. I kept focusing on God and loving my husband and children. By mid-July and the beginning of August 2021, I was known on social media and to some in my community as Ma, Hood Doula. It's a play-on-word, like My/Ma, because I'm also a mom. I was being asked to speak at events; I was featured on multiple accounts and platforms, especially as a Black doula because it's few of us in my city.

During that time, I was dealing with my youngest daughter's eczema flare-ups, and over-the-counter products didn't work. My husband and I weren't interested in using steroid-type skin creams. It was a lot, and I cried when she had no relief, scratching so much until the skin broke and bled. Our baby girl was suffering, so I broadened my study of herbs and took a deeper dive into the herbs I was familiar with. I came up with my own herbal blend to make herbal-infused oils that I used on our baby girl. My husband, children, and I, even my in-laws, witnessed our daughter's skin heal, and the scars disappeared. There was no trace of her ever suffering from eczema. I also changed my eating habits as I breastfed, and I removed certain foods from her diet because eczema is a gut health issue. I took pictures of her skin, documenting the results. I became pregnant and started using the oil on myself; in fact, our entire household used the oil and skin balms I made. After giving birth to our fifth and final baby girl, I shared our testimony and all of the pictures from the eczema flare-ups, the healed skin, and even the oil I used on our baby girl when the baby acne wouldn't clear. I had so many people who wanted to buy the oils and skin balms, which led me to create my herbal-infused body care and wellness products, "The Promise Body & Co." and my doula practice, "The Promise Doula Services."

Some people were surprised by many of the businesses my husband and I created, including things related to ministry. So many family members and friends have asked how we do it. How do we have time to create and operate while being parents, married, and having time for ourselves? The answer will always and forever be that we answer to God and get our strength from Him. No, we don't have all the answers; we are not perfect, but we consistently take everything to the Lord and let Him be God. We move at His pace, and even when I wanted to throw in the towel, God constantly reminded me why He needed me to walk in my purpose and His plan for my life. The Lord has made a way for us so many times and has been clutch in many situations, and I am so glad my husband believes in "Just GO." When God tells us to "Just GO," we GO. We don't have time to hesitate or question the plan.

I have learned I can make it or try to perfect it over time. As long as I GO, God will supply every need. I am so glad I said "Yes" to Jesus, said "Yes" to my husband, and said "Yes" to the call on my life. Every step in time was God-ordained; my life and our marriage, children, businesses, and ministry were all God-ordained. By trusting God, he made room for me to operate in my gifts and anointing, whether in my personal and business relationships or even the relationships/friendships I have cultivated in ministry. My life is not perfect by any means, but it's beautiful and worth living. When God tells you to Go, "Just GO."

In God, I have put my trust; I will not be afraid. What can man do to me? Psalms 56:11 NKJV

Facebook: MaHoodDoula
Instagram: @dawnlogo and @MaHoodDoula

Chapter 2

Daishanai Jefferson

The "Dai" I Lost My Mind

It was February 24, 2012, when I said, "I DO." I married my son's father. We had been together since July 14, 2004. During the beginning of our relationship, there were many red flags with him, all of which I ignored. What red flags, you ask? While we were in the early stages of getting to know each other, I was contacted by his child's mother on several occasions, stating he was yet in a relationship with her. It was my understanding that the relationship was simply a co-parenting one, not the relationship she was expressing. I first told him we could just call it quits; his response was, "So you're just going to take the word of another woman?" "Um… given you have a child with her, yeah, I am." I was not interested in this nonsense. I took him at his word, and we continued being friends.

We were okay with the understanding of our relationship until I got pregnant for the first time. Unfortunately, Alijah didn't make it. Dealing with the loss of our son, I needed some time to pull myself together. He gave me the space I needed. We were still together, but I was not emotionally available for him. It wasn't until the summer of 2005 that I noticed a change in his presence, and his availability shifted, another red flag. When I questioned him about it, he just said his hours at work had changed. I was so consumed with my job and raising my children that I wasn't really checking for him like that, meaning I was not going to check for receipts on what he told me, so we continued like that for several months.

It was Sunday, September 11, 2005, when my heart was shattered yet again. I received a phone call from his child's mother, she told me he got married on Saturday and not to her, mind you. I knew his behavior was off the way he communicated with me. The way he treated me was different. I was so naïve then that I was not paying attention to the signs (red flags) he gave me. Later, finding out this was the reason. He was entertaining another woman with whom he had established a full-on relationship. My "JACOB" and I talked. We shared our goals and dreams of what we wanted for ourselves as a couple and even made plans. We had a three-year plan that consisted of us moving in together and having our own family together. Have you ever met someone who got married on a Saturday and then slept with his girlfriend 48 hours later? Yeah, that would be me, the girlfriend.

He planted his seed on September 12, 2005; at the time, in my mind, that was it for us! He had married, and I thought we were done. Little did I know that day would continue his soul tie with me. I found out that I was expecting our second child together. I was in awe for many reasons. I thought of him, knowing this would be disappointing to him, considering he had a wife and a child on the way with her, but NO… To my surprise, he knew when I notified him, and he said it before I could even get it out of my mouth. At that moment, I felt, or should I say, I thought I was the winner; I won his heart, and I now have him. What should have been the end of us was merely the beginning. You see him, knowing he had not only one, but two babies on the way four months apart was merely his own twisted plan. You see, during our last intimate time together, the day we conceived our second child, he mentioned that we could still have each other, just me being a silent participator; needless to say, at that moment, I declined the suggestion.

Time passed, and that marriage did not last. See, what no one knew about me, "SPANKY," is that from the age of 18, all I dated were older men, so his being married did not defeat me; it put me back into an element I was familiar with. The only difference now was that I was emotionally invested in our relationship; I actually cared for him; I would even say I loved him. So, let's look at the facts: two failed marriages, and three kids later, I still said yes, I'll marry you. "Like Girl," how many more RED FLAGS does one person need? Well, let's just say it was not all love that had me saying yes.

Dai was in love with taking back what she thought was taken from her, to begin with. In addition to having a husband and not knowing what I was in for, in my understanding, I was doing good; why? Because, based on my religious beliefs, I was no longer shacking up and living in sin. I had no comprehension of what was ahead of me when I said, "I DO," and how much more SIN was to come not only by him but by myself as well. In my mind and heart, I finally got the chance to marry my son's father. I did not grasp that this man was my husband like in real life; it was no longer a game. We had been in our relationship for six years and were blessed with another chance at love and being parents.

The Word of God says not to be unequally yoked.

Do not be unequally yoked together with unbelievers. For what fellowship has righteousness with lawlessness? And what communion has light with darkness? 2nd Corinthians 6:14 NKJV

This started the mental disassociation of truth, love, honesty, commitment, loyalty, and faithfulness, and the list goes on, another "RED FLAG" my mind ignored. I was sold on the ring and all the significance it traditionally was meant to bring. I was captivated by the initial behavior of my "HUSBAND," now coming home to me every night, for now, that was. Many years have passed by, and a lot of our previous single lifestyle and character traits continued to surface from time to time; however, because we both were used to our uncommunicated, toxic ways and behaviors, we didn't address them. Instead, we just accepted it. That was just who we were, and we continued to perform as though things were all good in our home, with our children, family, and marriage. We even went to church regularly as a family. We were heavily involved in our church ministries as well as our children. Some would say we looked like we had it all together.

Remember, when you plant a seed, it will grow, especially when being watered, nurtured, and cared for regularly. This was what was happening. My husband planted the seed to take care of my "WANTS," to which he did an amazing job. Our children did not "want" for anything; however, what was missing was my "NEEDS," being cared for. My husband was taking care of my "wants," and my "needs" were being malnourished. So, I chose and found a way to nourish my "needs." When I had my "needs" met, I was not living in my right frame of mind. My mind let me think I was doing what was right for me. Making that decision was when I planted my seed of unfaithfulness. Due to my husband's actions and lack of communication, our minds started a war of toxicity towards each other. Our behaviors became a part of the destruction of our marriage. We unknowingly became more of opposers towards each other rather than a united front against what was happening in our relationship. This went on for many years. Wait, let me clarify this for you: we continued to love each other most unconventionally and traditionally known to humanity. My mind was so distorted; I was functioning off the vibes, feelings, and emotions I was digesting from him. I was so intoxicated with the illusion that this was my happiness that it became my everyday reality. We continued to be present as a family unit, but because we were so focused on our own selfish needs, our family and children were now being neglected by the lack of parenting and fulfilling responsibilities. Granted, they did exceptionally well in school and sports, but the nurturing, love, and teaching of good morals and values that we, as parents, should pour into our children were not being given to their fullest potential. I was barely functioning, with small attempts to exist in this world. My inability to want to acknowledge that I was slowly entering a state of depression was ever-present. However, I was in straight-up denial. My relationship with my children became distant; then, I became stagnant in all my relationships. I noticed I had no zest or zeal for life anymore. My husband was doing his own thing as usual; the kids were going and coming, and we stopped having family meetings, family outings, and even family dinners.

It was exactly 7:51 PM on Saturday, September 3, 2022. I experienced spiritual warfare within myself. I was fighting demons and did not know what was going on. I contacted one of my dearest friends, APOSTLE BONNIE, asking if she knew of any church services going on that night; I needed an outlet immediately. She replied that there was nothing going on that she was aware of, but I could call her. In the same text, she asked if I needed her to come over. I replied YES!!! Her next words were, "Send me your address. I'm on my way." She was at my house within 15 minutes. When she got there, I invited her in, and we were not even in the house five minutes when she said we had to loose the spirits in my house, so we opened the door and went outside. She started to pray over me, and just like that, I was on the ground; she continued to pray over me. I felt like a huge weight had been lifted off my chest, and I could breathe more regularly and with such ease. I was feeling dizzy as if I was hitting my head with a bat because the spirits that were consuming so much of me that when they left, I was unbalanced. It was in that life-changing moment "DAISHANAI" came back. Not knowing what would come of this recaptured freedom, all I knew was whatever God's intentions were for me, it would be a "YES" from me. I began attending church again and started making strides in my healing and forgiveness of myself, my children, my family, and my husband.

As of this writing, my husband and I have been together for 20 years and married for 12 years, yet we are still striving to restore and forgive each other. Every day isn't easy, but we, as husband and wife, have decided to intentionally desire to love each other better than we started.

Love forgives everything. Love is always trusting, and always hoping, and never gives up. 1 Corinthians 13:7

What a devil meant for evil, God meant it for our good.

You planned evil against me; God planned it for good to bring about the present result—the survival of many people. Genesis 50:20 CSB

God connected me with another longtime good friend, Nakisha B.K.A. "Coach Key." We had been going to church together for several months, and I would hear her talking about her coaching institute. I began asking more detailed questions. At the beginning of 2023, I joined her in

"Freedom to Blaze Your Trail." Given all that I have endured, God put it on my heart to establish a village of women to help those who needed support as I did, and in doing so, I am now the founder of the "UNDERGROUND SISTER CIRCLE," a women's support circle to help encourage, uplift, as inspire each other.

Contact me if you are interested in booking, teaching, coaching, and speaking events for a brand-new Dai.

Instagram: brandnewdai2023
Email: brandnewdai@gmail.com
Catch me on Facebook at Underground Sister Circle.

Chapter 3

Chermeka Alexander

Trust in God

Let us not grow weary or become discouraged in doing good, for at the proper time we will reap, if we do not give in. Galatians 6:9 Amp

Being asked to be part of "The Freedom to Blaze Your Trail" is an honor and blessing. I want to share with you the connection God ordained long ago for me and explain how He assisted me when I needed to trust in God to find my way back to Him. When Coach Key approached me about the book compilation, I had been in the coaching program for a year before I had agreed to be part of the book. I entered the Freedom to Blaze Your Trail coaching program in a season of difficulty dealing with the loss of my mother. I always put my faith in God, but this time, I was searching to understand why God had taken my mother from me, us, and the family. I was angry, lost, and looking for a way to escape the daily pain. I had isolated myself from my family, searching for understanding and comfort in the uncertainty of how I would face life without my best friend, my biggest cheerleader, my mom. I cried daily and prayed often but felt like I was so alone.

I had no idea the decision to take a ride would change my life. I decided that day to take a ride to a store a distance from my home to clear my mind and give me some time away. I prayed in the car and cried out to God that I needed direction. I was at a point where I did not have the remedy to fix, solve, or even acknowledge the depth of grieving a loved one brought. I was in a pain I could not begin to explain. I asked God for direction, a tribe, and resources to help me to heal. That day, I ran into Coach Key or, as I had known her, Nakisha. There at that moment, I was in a store with a childhood friend who knew my mom, could feel my pain, and see I was in need. In that meeting, Coach Key said after praying with me and exchanging contact information, "I have resources to help you; call me." God answered my prayer. A prayer I prayed just fifteen minutes earlier.

Do not fret or have any anxiety about anything, but in every circumstance and in everything, by prayer and petition (definite requests), with thanksgiving, continue to make your wants known to God. And God's peace [shall be yours, that tranquil state of a soul assured of its salvation through Christ, and so fearing nothing from God and being content with its earthly lot of whatever sort that is, that peace] which transcends all understanding shall garrison and mount guard over your hearts and minds in Christ Jesus. Philippians 4:6-7 AMP

On my ride home, I cried and thanked God and was taken aback in my spirit by how quickly the Lord had sent someone I trusted from my childhood. God knows me; I would not have received anyone I did not trust.

And the LORD, he it is that doth go before thee; he will be with thee, he will not fail thee, neither forsake thee: fear not, neither be dismayed. Deuteronomy 31:8 KJV

To give you a little back story, I always had my mother and was not raised with my father regularly in my life. It was always my mother, my little brother, and myself. I was raised knowing my mother's family but had an empty void of my father and his family.

I grew up going to church on various occasions, but I was not raised in Church. I did not understand the Bible, God, and my authority in Christ. There was no teaching of God except when referenced as present during a holiday or when I would talk with my great-grandmothers about reading their morning Scriptures.

It was rare for me to surrender myself or put faith in a space unknown. The unknown space for me was growing up not understanding the presence and peace of God in my life. God, as we know, is our Father, but with the absence of my father, it was hard to trust or put faith in a Father who was not seen and accept that He is the Lord. Trusting is not and was never one of my strong points, to be honest. I had been gifted from an early age with the gift of discernment. But I did not understand my gift, nor did I trust my gift.

I come from a good family, but like every family, there were family secrets, troubles, and issues that arose. My mom was always present, even through addiction, mental illness, and choices that did not always create the best results. My grandparents and mom's siblings played a huge part in my life. They were the extension of my mom, and the extension of my mom's family was the only family we connected with.

My mom and I were close, and she was present for many milestones in my life. As I mentioned, my mom was my biggest cheerleader, but sometimes, she could play my biggest adversary. We had a love-hate relationship; I prayed for the Lord to help her and me to have a strong mother-and-daughter relationship. I understood my mom to some extent and learned how to have a good relationship with her. I know it sounds a little strange but if you knew us you would understand. My mom was not perfect, and as I mentioned, she struggled but was always present. I have learned to understand and appreciate my mother's journey through life. I love her so much and am grateful for her as my mother.

The story of my life started long before 2005, but in 2005, I said yes to God and surrendered my life to Christ. I was baptized on Father's Day that same year. And yes, life began to change rapidly.

After I said yes to God, I began to develop faith through my experiences. Up to that point in my life, I had experienced betrayal in relationships, friendships, and family. I became a mother at 18 and was on an uncertain path I was not ready for. By the age of 20, I was living with my family, working part-time jobs, and my son was in the custody of his father. During my young adult life, I experienced emotional, mental, and physical abuse in relationships. This abuse manifested as manipulation, domestic abuse, sexual abuse, and wrong decisions that allowed different circumstances to arise. I had a gun put to my head by an abusive partner. I have been homeless, jobless, betrayed, neglected, rejected, and judged by family members because of my choices. The horrible emotions of shame, guilt, depression, doubt, unworthiness, and a sense of being lost would develop. I tried two times to take my life, but God had plans and purpose for my life.

As I stated, my life began changing with My Yes to God.
In 2005, God was making a way for me to get out of a relationship that had taken a huge toll on my life. I had no job after being fired and little luck in my search. I had been living with roommates, and because I was fired and did not have a source of income, I needed to move. I cried on the floor, lying on a pallet, and on the summer day when I was due to move, I had no idea where I would go. I prayed and cried. I was listening to Joyce Meyers on channel 58 in the afternoon. I called the prayer line, and Pamela prayed with me over the phone. Later that afternoon, my mom called to go and look for a place to move.

We moved into a one-bedroom apartment off 2nd Ave between 36th and 37th in Oak Park, Sacramento, CA. It was a place for my mom, brother, and me to have stability. I worked part-time for Starbucks as a barista and helped my brother and sister-in-law take care of my nephew. By January 2006, I had turned my attention away from the abusive relationship. I was finding myself and had a joy only God could bring to my life with the yes I had given Him. I worked over the years during my tough times to establish a solid relationship with my oldest son and made myself even more available to him. I would call every weekend and take every chance I could to visit him. By 2009, I had become a store manager with Starbucks and had my youngest son.

I can reflect on God's presence in my life at an early age, but I had not begun to put my faith in God and learn about Him. I could see where He covered me, but I had no idea that my life would still be filled with adversities, trials, and tribulations in saying yes to God. Out of ignorance, I thought my "yes" would deliver me entirely from all the bad and the hell I had been through, and it could never enter my life again. That would not be the case; however, I learned to obey God's Word and allow the Holy Spirit to guide me in my journey. Nothing in our lives is accidental, and God does not make mistakes. My "yes" came with work, and the work was necessary to guide me to the plan and purpose God has for my life. When I lost my job at Starbucks in 2010, I began going to school. I attended online classes and earned my bachelor's degree in business administration from American InterContinental University in December 2012. In my acceptance letter, I used the Scripture Luke 1:37: "For with God nothing shall be impossible."

I must say that learning about God and allowing the presence of the Lord in my life took breaking down walls. Walls I built around me to protect myself from the world. I had to learn to trust again. I had to learn that God was not of chaos or confusion, and over time, I developed the faith to trust in God. I was watching T.D. Jakes and listening to YouTube sermons online to continue building my faith as I faced adversity and being a single mother raising my youngest son.

I collected unemployment and other county assistance. Those were challenging times, but I learned to trust God in the uncertainty. Financially, if you have ever had to receive county assistance, you know there is no surviving to keep up with your household bills. I have no judgment about anyone having to receive help because that is what it's there for. It was challenging, but I thank God I no longer need county assistance.

In 2014, I began working as a Tax Technician for the State of California Franchise Tax Board. I was pleased to have a job that gave us financial stability and permanent employment. From 2014 to 2021, I focused on my family, raising my son, and caring for my mom since she had been having health issues. Over that time, I faced more adversity and tribulations; I continued to seek God, but not like before.

My focus and time had changed; I spent less time in the Bible, praying, or seeking the Lord and seeing the bright side of things. I had become distant from God. I was so caught up in the day-to-day living that I lost connection with my source, God. This was not God's fault but all on me. I had participated in faith-based groups, and my participation became less and less. I was not doing my daily devotions and not attending church or online church to get filled. I was hungry in my spirit. I also became complacent in my job and daily life responsibilities.

On February 11, 2022, I got the call my mom had been rushed to the hospital. I headed to the hospital to make sure my mom was well. Hoping I could take her home and help her recover. On the way to the hospital, I called to find out if she made it to the hospital and was informed my mom had passed away. To this day, I can replay in my mind the scream I let out when I heard I lost my mom. I had to go to the hospital and get my mom's possessions. I said my goodbyes. When I had to tell my brother, I became physically ill.

For the next four months, I grew angry, depressed, and increasingly isolated. I wanted no one to call on me for anything, absolutely nothing. I was okay to be left alone. I was facing days where I could not pick up the phone and hear her voice. She would not call and ask me what I was cooking or if I could come to pick her up. No more mom tagging along. No more mom, period. I had not realized how much my heart was hurting and longing for my mom.

In late June of 2022, I ran into Coach Key in the store. I called for the resources, and that is where we are today. Let me just say I am thankful. I am grateful to God and the forever presence of the Lord in my life. In my time of need on that day, I ran into Coach Key. I cried out, and the Lord heard my prayers even after my connection, by my own doing, had been less and less. I say this to say that in the tough times, I learned to stand on the Word of God, to keep my faith in the Lord, and to know in my spirit I always have a helper, the Holy Spirit. The Holy Spirit walks with me and shows me how to walk through life, knowing no matter what I face, I have help. Even if I walk physically alone, I do not walk alone. I come from a good family, but as we all know, every person has their journey. I made mistakes at an early age, fairytales narrated by society, and accepted the judgment of others about me. Now, I am standing on what the Lord says about me and the promises made over my life.

I am still working on breaking down the walls and trusting. I am far from perfect, but I thank the Lord for continuing to pursue me and never leaving me. The journey is much better with God than without Him. Some days are better than others because that's life. I know the Lord has freed me from believing lies that produced judgment and doubt. It's easy to get caught in the ways of the world. I thank the Lord for hearing me in my time of need and for the divine connection that was built years ago to be used years later. I am claiming the Freedom to Blaze My Trail by leveling up in life. I have been reminded of who I am in Christ.

I thank the Lord for my mom and the years I had her. She gave her best and never gave up, even in her struggles. I am learning to forgive the places where mistakes were made and give every person grace, including myself. I am thankful God has brought me through the fire, and I do not look like what I've been through.

Being associated with Coach Key, I have found a tribe of women I trust and have been working through my grief. The Lord has shown up every time I've gone to the workshops. The first workshop I went to would be a setup by the Lord. In the workshops, I was set free. My spirit had surrendered, and I needed it! The weight I had been carrying had become lighter. I now turn to the Lord daily for guidance and direction to help me serve those in need, whether my family, home, job, or community.

For I know the thoughts that I think toward you, says the Lord, thoughts of peace and not of evil, to give you a future and a hope. Jeremiah 29:11 NKJV

My plans and purpose are now to live a healthy, purposeful life for myself and love on myself through grace. As a certified life coach and keeping my faith and trust in God, I boldly develop and serve the community through the ministry W.A.L.K., Winning At Life's Kicks. We all face adversity in life, whether through self-choice or others. We all must celebrate our wins, whether big or small and trust the Lord through the process. Life can kick us all down, but when you put your faith in the Lord, read the Word of God daily, and pray, nothing with God is Impossible. God never turns his back on us, and there is nothing that can keep us from the love of God. I want to serve the community by providing resources to help set goals through motivation and mentoring, to encourage and support the achievement of their goals, and to help them celebrate their wins.

So, I encourage you to trust the Lord daily. I can testify and say it daily, "God will get the Glory in my story." The Lord has shown how faithful He would be in my life well before I acknowledged His presence in my life.

It is better to trust in the LORD than to put confidence in man. Psalm 118: 8 KJV

Trust in God and His plans for you, no matter what it looks like. The Lord is faithful!

Email: winningatlifeskicks@gmail.com

Chapter 4

Teiara Wortham

She Is Clothed with Strength and Dignity

When she speaks, her words are wise, and she gives instructions with kindness. Proverbs 31:26 NLT

For as long as I can remember, I have wanted to help others. I can remember when I was a small child, seeing commercials on television with little kids from Africa, and they would say only a quarter a day would help the children. I remember getting an envelope and a stamp, and I sent one dollar to the Feed the Children Ministry. That started my journey of helping others and pouring into them.

That journey hasn't been smooth. Coming up in the streets of Oakland was dangerous. We lived on one of the busiest streets, 90th Ave. Even at the age of ten, my life was really busy. I remember pumping gas with my younger cousins and little brother on 80th and East 14th Street. I saw that they were making money, so I joined them. That inspired me and stirred an entrepreneurial spirit in me, which is why I am who I am today. When I was around 11 years old, I met my best friend, Denise. Denise and I were inseparable. We did everything together; we dressed alike, took pictures, wrote poetry, partied, encouraged each other, and tried to do each other's hair. Denise introduced me to her cousin Kashana, and the day I met her, she moved in with us; we're still sisters today. Denise moved to Oakland from Los Angeles and was living with her father. Todd was strict and a man of God. He introduced us to the youth program at his church and made sure we were there at 6 o'clock every Tuesday. We loved the youth program so much that we went to church & joined the choir. We were there for about two years before her father passed away. He was our light in the midst of darkness. Denise and I separated when she went to a different high school.

In my first year in high school, I met another friend, and we bonded. Her father abused her, her sister, and their mom. I used to be so scared for her. I would go to her house, and her father would ask me for money to let her come outside. I remember I had gone over to her house on Halloween to see if she could go trick-or-treating, and her dad asked me if I had some money. I lied and told him no, but I didn't realize that he could see the money in my pocket with the shirt I had on. I still regret not giving him the money so they could come and trick-or-treat with us that night. Our family moved to West Oakland, California, to my aunt's house and that was the last time I saw my friend.

After living at my aunt's house for a few months, my parents moved us to Sacramento, California. I was so sad I didn't want to leave my hometown. Moving to Sacramento was a big culture shock; I had never seen mixed races together. Moving to Sacramento wasn't all bad, I met my boyfriend there and started attending church with his grandparents and family. I didn't understand what it meant to have a relationship with the Lord, all I thought was if I got up and went to church, I would be an angel, and everything would be perfect. One day, I met Sharitha, and she gave me some encouraging words that I have passed along to other women. She said I was beautiful, and when I look in the mirror, I should say, "I love myself better than I love myself, and no one can love me better." I added except God. The Lord is a healer and will deliver us from anything we can imagine. I didn't realize then how much I would need those words, or how I would need the Lord to be my healer and deliverer.

"Everyone you meet is fighting a battle you know nothing about. Be kind always"—author Robin Williams.

In 2010, at 30 years old I was going through a rough time in my life. My parents, who had moved back to Oakland, came to Sacramento to visit. I had asked my parents if they could come to get the kids. I was so stressed over life and the fact that my husband had been sentenced to ten years in prison, along with my younger brother. After they left, I ran some bath water and got into the tub with a bottle of pills. My phone rang. It was my little brother calling me from prison. He asked me what I was doing, and I remember crying, telling him I couldn't live life like this anymore. I felt so lost with no one in the world who could help me. My brother begged me not to end my life; he told me he was there for me and I had to be strong. He saved my life and many others that day. He didn't know it, but he held the key to my destiny. Many don't know or understand how valuable they are to others, how we can speak life or death into other's situations. The Lord saved me that day because He had bigger plans than I could ever imagine.

I began to meet women from different backgrounds, situations, and lifestyles. I opened my home to women who were having hardships and let them stay with me so they could get on their feet. I would always say yes, with no judgment. I did it even without understanding the situation I was putting my children in; taking their space and comfort zone. Everywhere I went, I was rescuing someone from a situation they were in.

I met a girl who was in foster care; her hair was matted, and she told me how people at school and at her group home used to tease her. I gave her my number and started braiding her hair, getting her things like hygiene and clothing to build her self-esteem. I also took my younger cousin under my wing, clothed her, did her hair, and built her up. While working at Motel 6 in a college town this tiny white female came to my window. You could tell she shouldn't have been staying in a motel. As I built a relationship with her, I talked her into leaving her pimp. I let her stay with me for about a week and then took her home to her mother. I never saw her again, but I talk to her occasionally. I met a lady from New Orleans who relocated because of Hurricane Katrina. She moved to Sacramento and ended up losing her children. I met her in the process of trying to get them back; however, because she was in an abusive relationship, they adopted her children out. She was so broken, and all I could do was offer her help and be a sister to her. During this time, I also served as a Sunday school teacher for the youth and volunteered at Saint John's shelter for women.

The Lord showed me how to treat people with love and respect. I didn't understand what the Lord was doing; I didn't completely understand His plan for me: to help build and pour into other women, to lift their self-esteem, and to love them unconditionally. I knew that sharing a little kindness would go a long way. The Lord has allowed me to have many daughters and sisters over the years, some for a season, some that have been in my life for twenty-plus years.

It's funny how I look back on things and laugh. That one dollar to Feed the Children Ministry sparked all of that so many years later. My ex used to say, "You're not Mother Teresa; stop trying to be like her." My other ex would say, "Man, that's what I love about you; you're always trying to save the world, but you can't TT. What are you going to have left?" I knew the answer: Freedom - I'm freed every time I pour into someone. Joy - I get happy knowing that the Lord is using me to empower other women who were broken like I was. Hope - I get hope knowing that all things are possible. I thank God for my parents because they didn't teach us the word NO; they taught us the word LOVE, and they showed us the meaning of unconditional love. I continued saying yes to showing love and in 2014, Sisters of Strength was born from a Facebook group to uplift women.

The acts of the flesh are obvious: sexual immorality, impurity and debauchery; idolatry and witchcraft; hatred, discord, jealousy, fits of rage, selfish ambition, dissensions, factions and envy; drunkenness, orgies. As I did before, I warn you that those who live like this will not inherit the kingdom of God. Galatians 5:19-21 NIV

Life was going well until it wasn't. I began living a Galatians 5 lifestyle, and I'm not talking about the Fruit of the Spirit. I downgraded from being a wife to someone's side chick. Love will take you on a rollercoaster ride; if we're not careful, we can find ourselves in a desolate place. On November 16, 2016, the day my husband and I separated, I found myself in that desolate place. My life changed forever because I allowed him to have a girlfriend. This wasn't the first time I had allowed him to do it. Back when I was pregnant with my daughter, I told him to find himself a girlfriend, and he did just that.

After the separation, I really couldn't see where my life was headed. Without direction, I had no hope, and my heart was broken. I walked away from my marriage to the man I thought I would spend forever with—a man I thought I would raise our grandchildren together, buy a house together, and grow old together. Everything I did was for my family, and now our family was torn apart. I fell into a deep depression, and the only person I could call on was the Lord. I prayed Philippians 4:13 over my life because I knew I could do all things through Christ, who strengthens me. I prayed daily.

Dear Lord, I have become the very person I thought I would never want to be. Truth is, I got myself in this position, and I pray that I can overcome the negativity I have put out into this world. Every day I wake up, I hope for a better day in life. I know that I must put more effort into doing positive things.

Dear Lord, I just want to thank you for everything I am going through; even though I can't see the result, I praise your name for allowing me and my family to see another day. Lord, I ask that You watch over my son and that Your will be done in his life and my daughter that Your will be done and not her will.

Dear Lord, I want to thank you for another day and another moment to give you praise. I ask that you continue to give me strength to move forward in my life. I don't understand what is going on, but what I know is you haven't bought me this far to leave me. Thank you for opening my eyes and heart; I just ask that you forgive me, Father, for all my wrongdoings. God, whatever your will is, Father, I ask that you continue to search my heart for the truth and allow me to turn from my wicked ways, in Jesus' name. Amen.

For I know the plans I have for you," declares the Lord, "plans to prosper you and not to harm you, plans to give you hope and a future. Then you will call on me and come and pray to me, and I will listen to you. You will seek me and find me when you seek me with all your heart. Jeremiah 29:11-13 NIV

God still had a plan for my life but as my journey continued, I went through so many trials and tribulations. Even with struggling with my own problems I continued to help others. I let my God-sent sister stay with me, and she was murdered the following month. I moved out of my place because when I walked into my house, I could still see her sitting on my couch clear as day, even though I knew she was with the Lord. My nerves were so bad, I didn't know if I was coming or going; every day was a blur. My thought process was so overwhelming I couldn't concentrate at work and I lost all three of my jobs. I became homeless and at rock bottom. As if all of that wasn't enough, a month later, my favorite auntie passed. Nothing could have prepared me for that day. Then a week later, my mom had a stroke, and two weeks after that, she had another one. Glory be to God, she made it through.

Dealing with so much trauma and loss, I fell deeper into depression. If my head weren't connected to my body, I would have lost it. I didn't care if I woke up the next day. I was so unhappy with my life that I truly didn't feel that the Lord cared about me anymore. It seemed as if my prayers were going unanswered, and there was no hope for me. The only thing I knew to do was to send a prayer up to the Lord. I constantly ask Him to help me and to guide me. I was desperately seeking the Lord. I didn't want to be in the situation I was in.

To everything there is a season, and a time to every purpose under the heaven: A time to be born, and a time to die; a time to plant, and a time to pluck up that which is planted; A time to kill, and a time to heal; a time to break down, and a time to build up; A time to weep, and a time to laugh; a time to mourn, and a time to dance; A time to cast away stones, and a time to gather stones together; a time to embrace, and a time to refrain from embracing; A time to get, and a time to lose; a time to keep, and a time to cast away; A time to rend, and a time to sew; a time to keep silence, and a time to speak; A time to love, and a time to hate; a time of war, and a time of peace. Ecclesiastes 3:1-8 KJV

I knew I would have to start all over again from scratch but I didn't anticipate this season being so long. Since I was still homeless, I was in desperate need of a place to live, so I subleased an apartment for about two months. When the landlord found out I wasn't the person who was supposed to be living there, I had to move. My nights were sleepless. I had nightmares; I was so stressed out. There was nothing I could do to make myself feel better. On top of that, my children's father got locked up again, so there was no option to send them to him.

I went to stay with my sister for a while then left my sister's house and went to stay with my brother; I was there for about a month. After I left his house, I went to stay at a hotel for a month. I still found no rest during this time. I moved to my other brother's house. His fiancé was sick, so I took her to doctor's appointments, did the grocery shopping, and cooked; she had me getting her house in order. We finished decorating her house, and four months later, she passed away.

I moved to my other sister's house in Elk Grove, CA. One night, about four in the morning, the kids came running in to wake me up, saying a tow truck was outside, about to tow my car. I went out, and yes, it was the repo man. He allowed me to get my things out of the car, but there was nothing else he could do for me. To make it worse, my son went to jail, and I now had to take care of his son. I continued to ask the Lord to help me and to guide me in the situation that I was in. I went back to my brother's house. I found a job, worked it for a couple of months, and saved my money.

One day the Lord told me to leave Sacramento and go to Marysville, CA. I didn't want to, but it was the best decision for me at the time. I packed up my belongings, and I moved to Marysville. I was so thankful I found a two-bedroom apartment. It was the following week of moving in that my neighbor asked me to give her a ride to church. It was Easter 2018, and I told her yes. I thank God for that, yes. That was the beginning of my breakthrough. As I was driving her to church, she described the pastor's character, how the Pastor was a woman, and how she had the Holy Ghost fire. I told her I would try to come another Sunday because I wasn't prepared, and I hadn't been to church in a while. That following week, I walked into service and was greeted with love and open arms. I felt like I was at home. The service was truly blessed, and I think I cried the whole time.

Trust in the LORD with all thine heart; and lean not unto thine own understanding. In all thy ways acknowledge him, and he shall direct thy paths. Proverbs 3:5-6 KJV

Just when I thought everything was finally falling into place, my daughter told me she was pregnant. I was in shock. I didn't see the signs, and I couldn't believe that my baby would be having a baby. I was embarrassed because I didn't want her to have a baby in her teenage years like me. I had so much hope and dreams for her future. I thought this just couldn't be happening right now. I told my daughter that she still had to finish school and we would have to make it work.

I needed the Lord to keep and love me because, at that time, I didn't know how to love myself or speak life into myself. Restoration Center Church, Pastor Ada Terry Aina, Spiritual Mom Hattie Evins, and Sister in Christ Kendra poured in and prayed for me like never before. I had a long journey ahead of me, but I knew I wanted to be on the Lord's side. Having daily conversations with my mother and reflecting on my life, she was constantly praying for me, and I know at times she was worried. I found a job at the mall driving the train and was promoted to manager two months later.

Fast forward, my daughter delivered a healthy baby girl and graduated at the top of her class. I enrolled back in school to get my high school equivalency diploma. Before the GED test changed, I only needed to complete English and I was done. But when my son got arrested, I had to either go to his court date or miss the test, and I chose his court date. So, all the hard work I had put in went down the drain, and I had to start at the beginning. After going to nineteen different adult schools and dropping out because either I didn't have a babysitter, had to move, or needed some money to pay bills, in June 2020, I walked that stage. Glory be to God. It took me three years, a graduation, and waiting on God to finally find rest and get some good sleep.

Dear Lord, I am asking for your blood to cover my family. Lord, please allow your will to be done in their lives. Whatever you want and ask any of us to do, we will obey you, your will, and your Word. Lord, I know there is a calling on my family, so I ask that you cover anyone connected to us with your blood. Lord, I ask that my family repent to you, choose you first, and get a relationship with you. Father, I pray for the spirit of obedience all over me and the spirit of faith, Lord; I ask that you give me patience and understanding in the name of Jesus. Father, I asked for the spirit of wisdom and knowledge over my life. Whatever your will is for me, I accept in the name of Jesus. Lord, allow your will to be my will. Let me see where you are working, and I join in. Lord, please remove any judgmental spirit from me; guide me with your eyes. Father, I ask that I serve you until the day that I die. Allow my flesh to die so that I may live in your spiritual realm doing your will, going where you tell me to go. In Jesus name, Amen.

I poured myself into church; I was not missing anything. I was on the prayer line at 5:00 in the morning. I started serving as a youth leader, ushering, on the pastor's aide committee, in the decorating ministry, and going out into the community, serving and praying for the people. I was on fire for the Lord. Whatever he called me to do, I started doing. However, I was still in love with my husband. He and I were still connected, which was one thing holding me back. I started asking the Lord to release me from him, and if it wasn't His will for us to be together, allow me to disconnect. It was one of the hardest things I ever had to do because even though he and I had our ups and downs and a lot of infidelities on both sides, I always chose him. I always put him first, and I always jumped to his call. I anchored myself in the Lord, I didn't want to play games with myself or anyone else.

The Lord started showing me gifts stored and hidden inside me.

I finally found myself and learned that I was a comedian. My stage name is Miss Parks, and she is the truth. Then, the Lord, let my Pastor allow me to put on a seminar called Women in Hats. The Lord used me in a mighty way to let women share their stories about drug addiction, obesity, prostitution, and entrepreneurship. Life was beautiful, God was turning my life around. We were doing things with the youth, and our women's ministry was growing. I began putting together events and when my Pastor was getting married, I put together her bridal shower. Then she came to me and said, "I think it's time for you to start your business." I was like, huh? She said it was time for me to start getting paid for my gifts and talents. I said, "No, Pastor, this is what I like to do. I don't like to charge people." She said it was time. Blast Off Events started the next chapter in my life.

For we wrestle not against flesh and blood, but against principalities, against powers, against the rulers of the darkness of this world, against spiritual wickedness in high places. Ephesians 6:12 KJV

I started doing parties, and then COVID-19 hit. I was sick from January 2020 to March 2020. I caught COVID, then the flu, and then COVID again. While at home, I saw a sister online promoting her coaching services, so I messaged her and said I was looking for a life coach. She referred me to Nakisha Woods.

When I met Nakisha, I was hanging on to two old relationships. When you're lonely and desire someone to love you, when someone gives you that attention you've wanted, it's difficult to turn away from them. I explained what was happening and how both were valuable to my life. One man built me up since I was fifteen. Every milestone in my life, he was there, including my graduation. The other was my ex, who I had been with since I was fourteen, and I wasn't ready to let go of him. Sister told me I had to leave them alone if I wanted to flourish. I wasn't trying to hear that because my husband and I were getting along well. He and I decided we would try it again, so I was looking for houses and found the perfect home. It was a three-bedroom, two-bath home, perfect for the grandkids to come and have their own space. I was so happy, I was getting my husband back. Many people rebel, yet they keep quiet about it because they want no one to look at them with disgust or be the topic of the conversation. Rebellion taught me that no matter what I do and how I do it, nothing will prosper from the situation if the Lord isn't in it, and it's not His will. All we're doing is prolonging our breakthrough when we turn away from the Lord. Plus, we live in shame and guilt because we know better. We also know the Lord wants better for us; however, we don't want to wait, so we spoil it for ourselves.

We were due to move on August 21, 2020, then boom, I got hit with a blow. The Lord said no. I couldn't understand, and I got angry at the Lord, but He let me see that even if I had all those things I wanted, my husband would not be there physically. He was only trying to make me happy, but he wasn't ready to settle down. I was so mad at the Lord; I was broken. I talked to my pastor and her husband, and I would be lying if I said I walked out of her office happy. I didn't understand how the Lord let this happen. I told my family and some of his family members, and I just knew things were going to be perfect. Nope. I fell right back into a depression, and I was so mad at God that I stopped going to church. I didn't want to hear anything about God because how could He allow this to happen? I am more embarrassed than anything because the Lord showed me a vision I was holding on to, and I let pride step in and destroy it. There was a lot of history, and I didn't want to break the soul ties keeping us together, but I knew what Nakisha was saying was the truth. So, I finally committed myself to stop dealing with both men.

I started traveling, something that I always desired. I went to Hawaii for five days, and every morning I woke up, I went to the water to spend some intimate time with the Lord. I asked Him for guidance and direction. I made the choice that I was choosing me, and I wouldn't allow myself to lay down with my ex anymore. I loved him so much that I had to release him and allow him to do what was best for him without my interference.

In 2021, on my birthday, I went to Miami. I will not lie my flesh wanted to have a good time, but our Father in Heaven said no. He blocked every avenue and path that led me to self-destruction. I didn't understand what the Lord was doing then, but now I give Him all the praise and the glory, for I don't know where I would be today. When I returned from Miami, I talked to my ex, who was more of an emotional support. We met up, and even though he was the same person, the feelings that I once felt had shifted. I saw the light, and the Lord was right there holding my hand. That October, I went on a cruise with my family to Mexico. I had my own space, so I laid in the room and wrote my words, but I was just so lonely; I was feeling empty inside and didn't know why. I wasn't talking to the men who had been a part of my life. It was mentally taking a toll on me, so I downloaded a dating app and met people here and there. Once I had a conversation with them, it was over. I went out on a few dates, but still nothing. That December, I went to New Orleans, and the more I went places, the more I started to learn who Teiara was. I began to know what I liked. I learned that I like to collect cups, and I love hats. I realized I didn't need a man to confirm my identity. I was still yearning for a relationship because that's all I knew. I learned that as long as I had the Lord on my side, that was who I was going to represent.

Then this message from the Lord came to me: "Family of Israel, you know that I can do the same thing with you. You are like the clay in the potter's hands, and I am the potter." This message is from the Lord. "There may come a time when I will speak about a nation or a kingdom that I will pull up by its roots or tear down and destroy it. But if the people of that nation change their hearts and lives and stop doing evil things, I will change my mind and not bring on them the disaster I planned. There may come another time when I speak about a nation that I will build up or plant. But if I see that nation doing evil things and not obeying me, I will think again about the good I had planned to do for them. Jeremiah 18:5-10 NIV

On November 4, 2021, God gave me a vision of a seminar called Wild Women Under Construction, and the reason for the name was because so many of us women are in the wilderness, not knowing what Satan has in store for us. Oftentimes, the Lord will show us what's not good for us, and because He is such a gentleman, He gives us a choice to do what's right. Our flesh makes us seek what is not good when our hearts and minds know what we should do.

Sickness started hitting my body from left to right: my stomach, headaches, my feet; I was going through so many problems I was at the hospital every week. I know now that The Lord was purging me of things I was hanging on to, and I had a lot of unforgiveness in my heart. I started praying different prayers for healing over my body. The Lord allowed me to release things and the bondage holding me back.

On May 25, 2022, my divorce was final. My ex and I talked on the phone that same day. I promise I was sad, but I was also ok with being free. In 2023, both my exes got married. Did it sting? Yes. But I pray for their marriages that the Lord will bless their union and lead them to a relationship with Him so He can guide them. The Lord let me start looking at the scenes where I was dishonest and harming myself and others. One thing about us humans is we forget that hurt people hurt people. My hurt stems from being raped at eleven years old; even then, I had a decision, and that hurt carried on for thirty years because I was looking for a protector. I was looking for love and validation; the answer was Jesus—the one who lived and died for our sins and rose three days later. I encourage anyone going through some deep hurt, grief, divorce, or depression to develop a relationship with the Lord.

Email: Teiarawortham@yahoo.com
Facebook: Teiara Blastoffevents
Instagram: @blastoffeventss

Chapter 5

ShaShanta Aldridge
Full Circle

When we hear the words FULL CIRCLE, we often think about when something or someone has 'circled back' around. In the Cambridge Academic Content Dictionary, it is defined as returning to a previously held belief or position. Coming 'full circle' can mean different things to different people. When God is orchestrating our 'full circle' moments, it is ALWAYS for our gain and for our benefit.

God never wastes a season! In Romans 8:28 we read that, 'All things work together for the good to them that love God, to them who are called according to His purpose.' What that tells us is no matter what we face in the seasons that we go through; it still falls under the 'ALL THINGS' so we have to then know that it's working for us. Even when it doesn't feel like it, we have to KNOW it is!

Full circle seasons are comprised of many full circle moments. Often, in our full circle seasons of life, we can extract and pocket valuable lessons, nuggets, and patterns from that season. This is why it's so important to remain 'students' in this thing called life. Being intentional about being a student of life automatically positions us to receive the gifts that keep on giving, also known as 'life lessons.

Full circle is so personal because I am in a full circle moment as I write this. Back in 2019, I made one of the hardest decisions I've ever had to make, which was to leave my almost 20-year marriage due to reasons outside of my control. I left the house that we had purchased one year before, the same house that I helped make a home. Simply put, I was devastated, disappointed, and downright scared. Why scared? I'm glad you asked. As someone who got married and said 'I do' at the young age of 20, from 20 to almost 40, all I'd known was marriage and how to be a wife. And just that fast, my entire life, as I had known it, changed and shifted right before my eyes! It was terrifying. To say I felt like a 'fish out of water' would've been an understatement, but I knew God was with me!

Being thrust into this new space called singleness was daunting, but because I understood that even in this, God was working behind the scenes and causing everything to WORK for my good, I knew that somehow, some way, GOOD had to come out of this.

Some would say that after being married for so long, I should've been excited about this newfound freedom that automatically came with being single. While that may have been true for some, the uncertainty and unfamiliarity made me feel stuck and unsure of what my future would look like.

My full circle season started January 1, 2020, when I heard the Holy Spirit say, the 'word' for you this year is HOPE! As I entered into this new year and season, I had to get my hopes back up! At that moment, the Lord began to show me that after experiencing disappointment after disappointment, I started to build up walls of protection by lowering my expectations of life and people. This was my way of 'guarding my heart,' or so I thought. I saw that since my 'hope tank' was so depleted, it was affecting my faith. I had to circle back and see those times when I was avoiding the feeling of rejection, disappointment, or let down; I would lower or remove my expectation that things would work out in my favor. The Lord began to show me that hope and faith go hand in hand. Hebrews 11:1 says, Now faith is the substance of things HOPED for and the evidence of things not seen. You cannot have faith if you refuse to hope! I clearly heard, to get all that I have for you, your hope and faith levels must match. I was reminded of the scripture in Proverbs 13:12 that says, 'hope deferred makes the heart sick' and Romans 5:5 that also says, 'hope will not make you ashamed.' At that moment, I accepted the challenge of getting my hopes up and breaking free from the spirit of disappointment!

Which brings me to the title of this book, 'The Freedom to Blaze Your Trail'. In order to truly be the trailblazer you were destined to be, you must first value and take full advantage of the freedom you were destined and created to walk in.

Freedom is defined as the power or right to act, speak, or think as one wants without hindrance or restraint. When we grasp the idea that the tests and trials we go through are there to make us stronger and help us build muscle, then and only then can we lead out the charge and set ablaze the paths set before us! We can walk down those roads of uncharted territory with confidence and find ourselves in the part of the scripture in the 23rd Psalm that says, 'Even though I walk through the valley of 'shadow' of death, I will fear no evil, for You are with me'! Sometimes, the unknown can feel like that 'valley of death' described there, but I'm grateful for His promise to us, to be with us and comfort us.

FREEDOM to Blaze Your Trail

What does it mean to be free? To embody freedom the way we were intended to, we must remember what it was once like to be bound and restricted, unable to walk in the fullness of ALL that's been spoken and declared over our lives! Then and only then can we appreciate what a blessing and opportunity it is to share our testimonies of freedom and let our stories set fire to the trails someone else will have to travel down behind us.

This freedom we've been given by God is not just for our benefit or for bragging rights. This freedom is like a contagious fire that ignites and blazes the trail for others that we're connected to. In Galatians 5:13 Paul tells us that we're called to freedom, not for our own selfish desires but to serve others. I encourage you today; embrace your freedom! Let anything that is trying to weigh you down fall off of you today! Allow the Holy Spirit to FREE you up and lighten your load. The Lord desires to free our minds, hearts, and souls from anything burdening us. Let's take a moment to do the 'burden exchange,' releasing every heavy burden and taking on His 'light burden.' In Matthew 11, God says, 'My yoke is easy, and My burden is light!' One thing is for sure: He will never put more on us than we can bear.

We've been FREED UP to BLAZE our trails!

Full circle moments provoke us to reflect. Looking back is not always a bad thing. Reflecting on what we've been through to extract the lesson is healthy. While living through my full circle season, I was determined to use that time of solitude as a time of intentional healing. That's when I saw singleness as a 'gift' and not a curse or demotion, and it started to transform me. When I became an active participant in the process designed for my growth and development, my healing journey kicked into overdrive! No matter how awkward and uncomfortable things started, I would be better for it ALL in the end.

Now take a moment, find a mirror, and tell yourself: Hello, Trailblazer! You were FREED for this!

Full circle moments have a way of forcing us to pivot or make a move. Most of the time, if we trace back to these moments, we'll see they were connected to a period of comfort and/or complacency. If we allow these God-orchestrated moments to unfold and play out, they can change the trajectory of our lives. Amazing things happen outside of our comfort zone. When you think about a 'pivot,' it means to turn, rotate, or spin, all while one foot stays planted without moving. The picture that paints for me is no matter how chaotic life gets. No matter how many twists and turns, God has a way of keeping us grounded and standing firm while leaving us flexible enough to circle back without losing our footing. We can trust Him to hold us steady in the turns of life.

Identifying full circle moments is essential. If you're not careful and if you're not able to read the room or recognize when you're in a moment, it can almost feel like you're revisiting the past or dwelling in what was when what you're doing is taking a second, and healthily assessing your experiences and pulling out the lesson you learned. Often, when we circle back, we're able to see something we didn't see before because we're able to view things from a new perspective and with different lenses. Take full advantage of your full circle moments and seasons. Remember, they are just moments that you're living and growing through, not your final destination.

Ultimately, there's a specific place for YOU! There are people, a village, a generation that speaks your language and needs everything that's been placed on the inside of you to come forth in its FULLNESS! We're in a time where it seems like everything goes, and the standard has been lowered to make it convenient. But there's a remnant that's been fashioned, created, and designed for such a time as this! You're hidden in obscurity, being cultivated and prepared. Everything that you experienced on the backside of the mountain when it felt like no one could 'see' you. When it felt like literal isolation, when you felt you weren't 'findable,' All of that was orchestrated to process and develop you! To shield and protect you from the potential of further damage and being mishandled when you were most delicate. Like film in the dark development room, He kept you hidden as you were being processed to reduce unnecessary fingerprints and damage from exposure to light too early. Remember, God never wastes a season! He makes it all count! His math skills are second to none. He will take the additions and subtractions of our lives, divide them up, balance us out, and cause our lives to do exactly what He told us to do in Genesis 1:28: be fruitful and multiply!

I encourage you to SPEAK LIFE over yourself daily. No matter what you may see in your full circle moment, commit to only speaking what God said about you! Words have the power to create! Words can make or break a season; they can fuel or frustrate; accelerate or aggravate a season. Choose your words wisely when navigating your full circle seasons!

Let's pray:
Father, we thank You for life! We thank You for every full circle season and moment You've orchestrated in our lives. We thank You for how

You have uniquely created us to be who we are. We thank You for freeing us from every hinderance and stumbling block intended to stop and keep us stuck. We get in agreement with every word You've spoken over us! We change our language today. We speak life to any area where the 'shadow of death' may have tried to loom over. Cause our words to propel us and pull us out of the state of being spiritually paralyzed. We declare LIFE to every purpose and plan You've placed in us! Thank You for breathing Your breath of life in us and resuscitating every gift lying dormant and lifeless! We declare in this moment, there's a PULSE! In the Name of Jesus, we pray! We believe it to be so! Amen.

Email: shespeakzlife@gmail.com
Instagram: shespeakzlife
Facebook: ShaShanta Aldridge
TikTok: @shespeakzlife

Chapter 6

Nakisha Woods

Honor Your Yes

Thank you so much for honoring your yes by investing in yourself by reading our book. I was going back and forth on whether I would submit a chapter in The Freedom to Blaze Your Trail Volume I Level Up Edition.

Then I heard the voice of the Lord say you must write about honoring your yes.

Honor Your Yes started as a live on Facebook. I sat on my room floor and the Holy Spirit began to download and reveal the power of honoring our yes. I received so many comments on how the topic was freeing many of my Facebook friends. The live was authentic, transparent, and convicting. I was totally open and real. I had not been honoring my YES! I was begrudging my YES. Have you ever been there before?

You give your yes to go to an event; however, on the day of the event, you are tired, frustrated, and just can't get it together. Then what happens? It begins to show up in your attitude. You show up late, looking unprepared. Why? Because you did not honor YES. I have identified five keys to honoring your yes and would like to share each of them.

However, first, let's define honor. According to the Oxford Dictionary, honor is defined as follows

noun

high respect; great esteem. to what is right or to a conventional standard of conduct.

verb

regard with great respect.

fulfill (an obligation) or keep (an agreement).

Let's dive a little deeper. A verb is an action word. To regard with great respect and fulfill an obligation is an action word. When you put honor into action you must regard your YES with great respect. It becomes a movement! Saying yes is an action that must be regarded and respected. When we say yes to our coaching practices, going back to school, or being in a relationship it should not be taken lightly.

🗝 1st Key

As soon as an opportunity arises, you get an idea (I like to call ideas visions) I would encourage you to pray for wisdom and guidance before you even YES. Take it to the throne. Ask God if this is something He is desiring you to do. Is it something that aligns with the season in your life?

I urge, then, first of all, that petitions, prayers, intercession and thanksgiving be made for all people—for kings and all those in authority, that we may live peaceful and quiet lives in all godliness and holiness. 1 Timothy 2:1-2 NIV

During your prayer thank God for the opportunity and the inner strength to let you complete each step associated with your yes. When we take it to our Father who art in heaven all things will align. Everything that is associated with your Yes will work in your favor. Always remember God never makes a mistake. Even if things are hard when honoring your yes you must remember that.

And we know that in all things God works for the good of those who love him, who have been called according to his purpose. Romans 8:28 NIV

Be encouraged that God is working things out behind the scenes. Honoring your YES requires faith in action. It requires you to not waver when things get rough, but to trust in God. After all, you prayed and got the OK. God's hands and will are wrapped around you, honoring your YES.

2nd Key

Forgive yourself and others for any offenses that may have accrued before you honored your YES.

Forgiveness is such a vital part of our success in any area of our lives. We must forgive and release ourselves and others from the dungeon of unforgiveness. It is essential in honoring your YES. You cannot honor your YES while harboring resentment, shame, and pain. Remember part of the definition of honor is fulfill and regard with great respect, it is challenging to do that if you have unforgiveness lingering in your heart.
When you honor your YES, please release yourself from the dungeon of unforgiveness and bitterness.

Bear with each other and forgive one another if any of you has a grievance against someone. Forgive as the Lord forgave you. Colossians 3:13 NIV

For example, you may have committed to building your coaching practice. You were all excited and had all these great ideas, but then BOOM! A financial barrier tries to come against your coaching practice, and your funding and resources dry up. You begin to resent yourself, and distorted thoughts take over your mind—thoughts like" I knew I was not good enough to build a successful life coaching practice."

If you can relate, please forgive yourself and all your thoughts associated with the financial barrier. Release yourself and move forward with grace and love.

Many successful entrepreneurs make big mistakes; however, they do not give up. And neither will you. Forgive yourself and keep it moving.

3rd Key

Celebrate your Yes.

Anytime you say YES, especially to your OWN business, going back to school, or increasing your professional development, please saturate YOUR YES with love, excitement, and enthusiasm.

If you approach YOUR YES with dread, doom, and gloom, you are liable to get that response from the situation you said YES TO.

Treating and celebrating your YES can be simple things like having a theme song you listen to each morning. You can affirm your YES by creating affirmations that support your YES.

Also, taking good care of your body is a way to celebrate your YES by going to bed at a decent hour, creating a healthy diet, and exercising as well.

4th Key

Seek an accountability partner with your best interest at heart and who would like to see you WIN.

Examples:

• Accountability Partner - a trusted individual who will hold you accountable for meeting your goals.

• An Empowerment Coach - a coach who is an expert in empowerment.

• A Person you admire- this person could be a family member, col-

league, or church member
• An expert in the area you said yes to. For instance, if you said YES to becoming a fitness coach, find an expert in that area to follow and shadow.

5th Key

Honoring YOUR YES TO YOU means sometimes saying NO!
Please be ok with saying NO!

Often, when saying yes to something you already feel will be too much, you have done a disservice to yourself, so please seek wisdom before saying yes.

It is okay to set boundaries. The first YES we must honor is the YES to ourselves in all areas of life: spiritually, physically, and mentally.

This lets us walk in the true victory and freedom to blaze our trails!

If you are interested in any of our services, please subscribe at www.keys2victory.com

Honoring your YES gives you the Freedom to Blaze Your Trial.

Acknowlegments

First giving honor to God who is the head of my life. Thank you heavenly father for our relationship and friendship. Thank you for choosing me as a vessel to birth such an amazing project. You have never left me or forsaken me.

Second I would like to thank my mother Natalie Gibson and each of my daughters I refer to them as my sparkling gems Alonie, Bobbi, Brea, and Blessette.

Mommy thank you for supporting me and believing in me even if you didn't understand this project, you still supported me. I will not forget that. It was soft support like cleaning the kitchen, cooking meals during the time of the book launch and giving me my space to create. I love you mommy and am so thankful for you.

Alonie as my first born you have attended so many of my workshops and have assisted me in numerous ways. You are my first born and my reason why I began to do my healing work. Bobbi, you have always been with me building programs throughout my career. When Keys2Victory was birthed, you were right there supporting listening to my ideas and so forth. Brea the day of the book launch you were up early excited and eager to serve with your mother. I appreciate you daughter. To Blessette my youngest miracle baby thanks you for sharing me daughter thank you for being such an easy gentle soul and spirit.

I would be remised if I did not acknowledge my Aunt Nancy who seen the gift of counsel, coaching, and encouragement in me when I was sixteen. I still remember our conversation. You asked for my advice, after I advised you, you yelled out loud "Kisha you are a counselor!" Your words poured into my inner-spirit and allowed to soar and rise as the powerful life empowerment coach I am today.

All my family is very important to me and has supported me in one way or another. However, I have some very special individuals who have supported me in above and beyond measures. My brother Tyrone Anderson has always pushed me and was one of the first people to say "Sis when you speak, we listen". I was scared when you first said that to me bro. However, now I know God was using you to pour into me. I have two cousins that serve as my best friends Shawntae Wright and Selena Richardson. Cousin Shawntae thank you for the encouragement and the push for me to go back to school to obtain my undergrad. Your boldness, courage, and resilience are transformable. I appreciate you. That was a huge deposit in my spirit amongst so many more. Cousin Selena, all the conversations and the edits to my bio, your ideas that have helped me through this journey of entrepreneurship has not gone unnoticed. I appreciate you.

To my cousin Keenan owner of K.I.M.V. LLC, clothing company thank you for your support cousin, watching you soar is such a blessing. To my neicy Iyanna Jennings owner and founder of Nouvelle Healing, niece I thank you for all your innovate ideas, your photographs, for you always seeing the best in your auntie, I love you and am very proud of you.

In my processing of thanking God for all that have supported me through the years, I must say that without my inner circle prayer team the Apostles that cover me, counsel me, teach me, and love me unconditionally Apostle Tuesday Nolden of Complete in Him International Ministries and Apostle Bonnie Hale of #SET FREE Deliverance Ministry. I would have been left uncovered on some of my most challenging days. These two anointed Apostles demonstrate what Scripture says, ***"As iron sharpens iron so one person sharpens another." Proverbs 27:17 NIV***

I did not grow up in church. I have only been a member of two churches in my entire adult life. I would like to say thank you to the shepherds of each congregation and their families.

The first church I became an active member then servant leader was Antelope Upper Room Ministry "A Shelter from the Storm", Pastor Juanita Mason a.k.a Yoke Breaker, Sacramento, CA. Thank you, Pastor Mason, for your unwavering dedication to teaching and preaching the gospel to us. It was under your leadership where I heard the call upon my life.

The second church I am a current member and Children/ Youth Pastor is Arden Church of the Nazarene Pastor Jim Dorsey. Pastor Jim has planted and developed churches across the United States. I have served under Pastor Jim's leadership for the last seven years. I have learned and developed so much as a mature believing dedicated woman of God. I thank you Pastor Jim and your entire family.

Thank you to my first coach, Sheya Chisenga, The Woman Christian CEO, mighty woman of God. I thank you for your YES! Your boldness. Your continued evolution. You have been an enormous inspiration in my life and my coaching practice. Denise Johnson, owner and founder of DSJ Design. Denise designed our book cover and continues to blow my mind with her gift of prophetic creativity.

In closing TRAILBLAZHER's Pastor Mason, Dawneshia Logo, Daishanai Jefferson, Chermeka Alexander, Teiara Worthham, ShaShanta Aldridge a huge THANK YOU my beloved sisters for your prayers and trusting the God in me. A delay is never a denial. You are all so very special to me and I have been privileged to witness the growth and elevation in each of you powerful treasured beloved vessels of the Lord.

"You are the salt of the earth. But if the salt loses its saltiness, how can it be made salty again? It is no longer good for anything, except to be thrown out and trampled underfoot. You are the light of the world. A town built on a hill cannot be hidden." Matthew 5 13-14 NIV

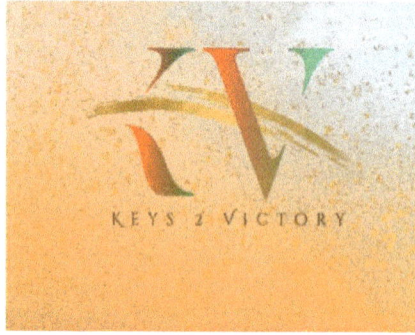

www.keys2victory.com

Apostle Nakisha Woods, known as Coach Key, serves the world, fulfilling her passion and purpose, guiding people to walk in their victory. She is a mother, pastor, entrepreneur, mentor, motivational speaker, and author.

She uses her influence to mentor people worldwide through her coaching programs, 90 Days 2 Your Victory and Freedom 2 Blaze Your Trail Book Analogy. Coach Key is an advocate for domestic violence survivors, at-risk youth, and adult education students across the country.

Coach Key also serves as Legislative Chair, Northern Section, for the California Council for Adult Education. Coach Key is a servant leader dedicated to serving people.

Coach Key is a true worshiper and intercessor after God's own heart, a testament of God's restoration and redemption power.

She is an Apostle and serves at Keys2Victory Ministers in Sacramento, CA. She is the proud mother of four beautiful daughters whom she refers to as her "GEMS": Alonie, Bobbi, Brea, and Blessette.

Milton Keynes UK
Ingram Content Group UK Ltd.
UKHW051854281024
450367UK00019B/299